D0460690

# OUR GREAT STATES

## WHAT'S GREAT ABOUT
# MONTANA?

✳ Darice Bailer

⌐ LERNER PUBLICATIONS COMPANY ✳ MINNEAPOLIS

# CONTENTS

Content Consultant: Keith Edgerton, PhD,
Chair, Department of History
Montana State University–Billings

Lerner Publications Company
A division of Lerner Publishing Group, Inc.
241 First Avenue North
Minneapolis, MN 55401 USA

For reading levels and more information, look
up this title at www.lernerbooks.com.

Main body text set in ITC Franklin Gothic Std
Book Condensed 12/15.
Typeface provided by Adobe Systems.

Library of Congress Cataloging-in-Publication
Data

Bailer, Darice.
    What's great about Montana? / by
Darice Bailer.
        pages    cm. — (Our great states)
    Includes index.
    ISBN 978-1-4677-3387-8 (lib. bdg. :
alk. paper)
    ISBN 978-1-4677-4712-7 (eBook)
    1. Montana—Juvenile literature.  I. Title.
F731.3.B27  2015
978.6—dc23                    2014001997

Manufactured in the United States of America
1 - PC - 7/15/14

# MONTANA Welcomes You!

Have you ever seen a wild grizzly bear? Looked up at the scary jaws of a *Tyrannosaurus rex*? Or watched a team of yipping huskies race past you in the snow? Take a trip to Big Sky Country. You can see all those things here! In Spanish, the word *Montana* means "mountain." Take a boat ride on a lake in Glacier National Park. You'll see why the state earned its name. Breathtaking mountain views surround you. If you like outdoor adventures, history, and fun, Montana is the place for you! This vacation spot is waiting for you to discover it. Read on to learn about ten fun things you can do in Montana!

CANADA

Kootenai National Forest

Glacier National Park

Kalispell

ROCKY MOUNTAINS

Havre

Clark Fork River

Flathead River

Missouri River

Great Falls

Missoula

Helena

Anaconda

Butte

Big Hole River

Belgrade

Bozeman

Billings

Yellowstone River

Miles City

Granite Peak (12,799 feet/3,901 m)

IDAHO

WYOMING

NORTH DAKOTA

SOUTH DAKOTA

N

Miles
0   20   40   60
0   40   80
Kilometers

Explore Montana's mountains and all the places in between! Just turn the page to find out all about BIG SKY COUNTRY. >

# MONTANA DINOSAUR TRAIL

> Do you like studying dinosaurs? Well, there's no better place in the world to do that than Montana. Millions of years ago, Montana was very different. It was warm and swampy. Many dinosaurs lived here. In fact, paleontologists have found more kinds of dinosaur fossils in Montana than in any other US state. Hit the famous Dinosaur Trail to learn more about these amazing discoveries!

The trail takes you to fourteen different locations across the state. Each location is full of exciting facts about dinosaurs. Make sure to pick up a passport at one of the museums or online. Then get the passport stamped at all the locations!

Start at Bozeman's Museum of the Rockies. You'll see the largest *T. rex* skull ever found.

Do you dream of being a paleontologist? You'll get the chance to dig for fossils at the Great Plains Dinosaur Museum and Field Station. This museum outside Malta offers summer programs geared toward kids.

Fossil hunters search for dinosaur bones at one of the stops on the Dinosaur Trail.

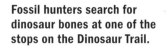

The Museum of the Rockies has one of the largest fossil collections in the world.

LEWIS AND CLARK TRAIL

# LEWIS AND CLARK
# NATIONAL HISTORIC TRAIL

> No trip to Montana is complete without a visit to the Lewis and Clark National Historic Trail Interpretive Center. This fun museum is in Great Falls. Here you'll learn what life was like for two of the United States' most famous explorers.

Start in the center's theater. What nearly pushed American Indian translator Sacagawea into the Missouri River? Did the grizzly bear chasing Meriwether Lewis ever catch him? A twenty-minute film will tell you the answers!

Learn how the explorers talked to American Indians. Find out if you're strong enough to pull one of the explorers' canoes against the river current. Then head outside to hike one of the center's many trails.

Summer is a great time to visit the center. Spend your morning at the river camp. Guides will teach you how to make a fire with flint and steel. Then learn how to find your way with a compass.

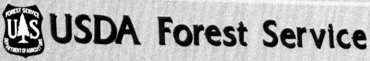

## WHO WERE LEWIS AND CLARK?

In January 1803, US president Thomas Jefferson ordered an important expedition. The United States was in the process of buying a huge section of land. This land made up what is now the western United States. Jefferson wanted a group of men to explore it. Meriwether Lewis and William Clark led the expedition. From 1804 to 1806, Lewis and Clark traveled from Missouri to the Pacific Ocean and back, crossing Montana.

# LITTLE BIGHORN BATTLEFIELD

> The Little Bighorn Battlefield is a stop you can't miss on your tour of Montana. This quiet field was once the site of one of the nation's most famous battles.

As you stand in the field, try to imagine what life was like for the people involved. Try to hear the cries of the Sioux and Cheyenne warriors. Can you feel the thunder of horse hooves?

Look for the monument to Lieutenant Colonel George Custer and his men. Across the street is the Indian Memorial. This honors the American Indian warriors who lost their lives.

Stop by the Custer Battlefield Museum. Here you'll discover what life was like for American Indians on the Great Plains. American Indian weapons from the 1800s are on display inside. You can also see clothing the Plains American Indians might have worn in battle.

A monument honors the US soldiers who were killed in the Battle of Little Bighorn.

## THE BATTLE OF LITTLE BIGHORN

In 1876, the US government ordered American Indians living in Montana to move to reservations. The American Indians did not want to leave. Lieutenant Colonel George Custer and his men tried to drive the American Indians onto the reservations. From June 25 to June 26, a battle took place. More than one thousand American Indians fought approximately six hundred US soldiers. The American Indians won the battle. But within a few years, the US government forced American Indians to live on the reservations.

# CROW FAIR

> The Crow Fair near the Little Bighorn River is a wonderful way to learn about Montana's American Indians. It is held in southeast Montana in the third week of August. The fair is five days long. It is one of the largest American Indian gatherings in the nation. All are welcome!

The air is filled with the sound of beating Crow drums. You can also hear Crow people sing in their ancient language. See Crow men, women, and children dressed up in bright, colorful clothing. They wear feathers, beads, and moccasins. Not far away, more than one thousand tepees are set up. American Indians from around the state camp in these tepees.

The fair begins with a colorful parade each morning. Don't miss the rodeo later in the day. American Indian cowboys and cowgirls rope calves and wrestle steers. Then check out the horse races.

The fair ends with a parade dance. Drums bang and everyone dances around the powwow grounds.

A cowboy competes in a cow-tie event at the Crow Fair.

## THE CROW PEOPLE

The Crow people call themselves *Apsaalooké*. That means "children of the large-beaked bird." At one time, the Crow lived in a huge area of central Montana. Now most live on the Crow Reservation in southern Montana. The Crow are one of many American Indian nations that call Montana home.

# GLACIER NATIONAL PARK

> Glacier National Park is a great place to visit if you like wild animals. The park is home to grizzly bears, mountain goats, and more. Keep an eye on the sky. You might catch a glimpse of a bald eagle. The park is known for its amazing glaciers. You can even have a snowball fight in summer! Snow sticks to the park's glaciers year-round.

Start your tour on Going-to-the-Sun Road. The road takes you through the heart of the park. It is open only from June to September. The rest of the year, it's buried in snow. Look for wildlife on the roadside. You may see a moose munching twigs. Keep an eye out for bighorn sheep with curled horns. You could even spot a black bear and her cubs!

Afterward, go rafting down Flathead River. You'll bounce over river rapids named Jaws and Bonecrusher. You can also hike or go horseback riding.

In the winter, be sure to ski on the slopes. The area around the park offers six downhill ski areas. Take in the stunning scenery as you fly down the mountain.

Moose *(left)* and bighorn sheep *(below)* both live in Glacier National Park.

# GRIZZLY AND WOLF DISCOVERY CENTER

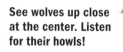

See wolves up close at the center. Listen for their howls!

> The grizzly bear is Montana's state animal. And there is no better place to see grizzlies than at the Grizzly and Wolf Discovery Center in West Yellowstone. This is a wildlife park and educational center.

Here you can meet and learn about grizzly bears. The center also has two packs of gray wolves. Look through the window of the center's Naturalist Cabin to watch the wolves in action. Can you pick out the pack's leader?

The center takes care of orphaned grizzly bear cubs. Watch the cubs wrestle, roll in the snow, and fish. The center is also a safe place for adult grizzlies. It takes in bears that are no longer able to live in the wild.

During summer, be sure to take part in the center's Keeper Kids program. Learn what grizzly bears eat. Then go into the bear habitat. You can help an animal keeper hide food for the bears. Animal keepers let the bears back into the habitat after you leave. Watch the bears find the food you just hid!

The Grizzly and Wolf Discovery Center
is full of fascinating information
about wolves and grizzly bears.

17

# RACE TO THE SKY

> Montana's Race to the Sky is for dog lovers. This exciting dogsled race takes place every February.

Watch the Junior Race for young mushers. It is for teens who are fourteen to seventeen years old. The 100-mile (161-kilometer) race starts in Lincoln. See the sleds hitched to a dozen Alaskan Huskies. Watch the drivers yell "Ready, Hike!" as they take off. Hear the dogs yelp. They are pulling as hard as they can.

The 350-mile (563 km) adult race starts near Helena. You can cheer for the racers near the starting gate. Make sure to head to the finish line in nearby Lincoln. You'll want to clap for the winner!

Would you like the chance to ride on a dogsled? Many companies throughout Montana's mountains offer dogsled rides. Experienced guides drive the sled. You can kick back in a comfy seat as you fly across the snow.

Many dogsled companies offer dogsled trips where you can meet sled dogs and ride on the sled yourself.

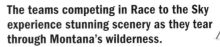

The teams competing in Race to the Sky experience stunning scenery as they tear through Montana's wilderness.

19

# GRANT-KOHRS RANCH

> Have you ever wondered what it's like to be a cowboy or to live on a ranch? Find out at the Grant-Kohrs Ranch National Historic Site in Deer Lodge. Grant-Kohrs was Montana's first ranch. A cattle trader built a house here in 1862. He began selling beef to hungry miners. Grant-Kohrs is still a working ranch.

Check out the old bunkhouse where the cowboys slept. Sit down in front of a chuck wagon. A park ranger will tell you all about life on the range. You can even try on some cowboy clothes.

Be sure to check out the ranch's many summer programs. You can learn how to build a tepee or cook over a campfire. The Pioneer Skills class is extra fun. It will show you what chores were like for kids in the 1800s. The Who Pooped at the Ranch? class teaches you how to look for clues in animal poop. What animals scampered across the ranch? Their poop will tell!

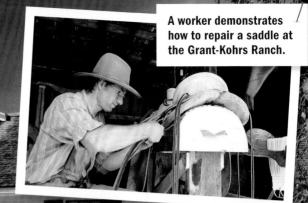

A worker demonstrates how to repair a saddle at the Grant-Kohrs Ranch.

## RANCHING

Cattle ranching is one of Montana's most important industries. Cattle ranchers were drawn by Montana's grassland. It was the perfect spot for their cattle to graze. Cattle ranching is still common in the state.

# WORLD MUSEUM OF MINING

> Learn what life was like for a miner at the World Museum of Mining. This exciting museum is in Butte. Climb into a cage that miners rode 2,700 feet (823 meters) down each day! Then ride down yourself. An underground mine exhibit is waiting for you. Don't forget your hard hat and headlamp. It's dark down there!

Afterward, peek into an old mining village. Hell Roarin' Gulch is a replica of a mining town from the 1890s. It still has the old schoolhouse, the jail, and the general store. Check out the old miner tools in the mine yard! This exhibit is full of mining equipment.

See what it may have been like to work deep inside a Montana mine at the World Museum of Mining.

## MINING

Mining was Montana's first big industry. In 1862, prospectors found gold in a creek. Miners found silver and copper in the state too. Men rushed to Montana to get rich. Many mineral resources can be found in the state's mountains. Montana mines still turn out copper, gold, silver, platinum, and lead. In fact, the state's motto is *Oro y Plata*, which means "Gold and Silver" in Spanish.

23

# MONTANA PARKS

> Montana's many parks are a great way to experience nature. Did you know that Montana has more wildlife than people? One of the best places to see Montana's wildlife is at the National Bison Range. This is a refuge for bison near Dixon. Bring your camera. You'll want to snap pictures of the huge animals grazing. In the spring, keep an eye out for adorable calves. Deer and antelope are also common on the range.

Before you leave Montana, visit the Kootenai National Forest. The forest is known for many beautiful hiking trails. You can walk across the swinging bridge that crosses Kootenai River Gorge. Look down if you dare! You'll see the Kootenai River gather speed and surge over Kootenai Falls. After your hike, throw a fishing line in the river. That night, snuggle up in your sleeping bag in one of the forest's campgrounds. Don't forget to do some stargazing before turning in!

Drop a line in the beautiful Kootenai River *(top)* to see if you can catch some rainbow trout. If you dare, hike across the swinging bridge at Kootenai Falls *(right)*.

## YOUR TOP TEN!

You've read about ten awesome things to do and see in Montana. But what would your Montana top ten list include? What would you like to see and do if you visited Big Sky Country? What attraction has you the most excited? These are all things to think about as you write your own top ten. After you write down your top ten list, turn it into a book. Illustrate the book with drawings or pictures from the Internet or magazines.

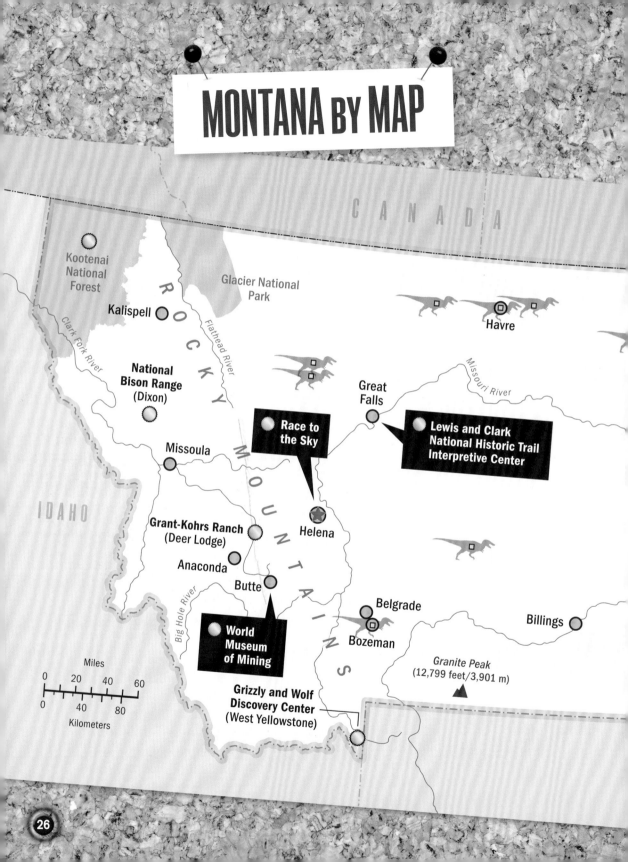

# MONTANA BY MAP

CANADA

Kootenai National Forest

Glacier National Park

Kalispell

ROCKY

Flathead River

Clark Fork River

National Bison Range (Dixon)

Havre

Missouri River

Great Falls

**Race to the Sky**

**Lewis and Clark National Historic Trail Interpretive Center**

Missoula

IDAHO

M
O
U
N
T
A
I
N
S

Grant-Kohrs Ranch (Deer Lodge)

Helena

Anaconda

Butte

Big Hole River

**World Museum of Mining**

Belgrade

Bozeman

Billings

Granite Peak (12,799 feet/3,901 m)

Miles

0   20   40   60

0   40   80

Kilometers

Grizzly and Wolf Discovery Center (West Yellowstone)

Capital city

City

Point of interest

Highest elevation

International border

state border

Montana Dinosaur Trail site

MONTANA

ORO PLATA

Visit www.lerneresource.com to learn more about the state flag of Montana.

N

Yellowstone River

Miles City

Little Bighorn Battlefield (Crow Agency)

SOUTH DAKOTA

WYOMING

# MONTANA FACTS

**NICKNAMES:** The Treasure State, Big Sky Country

**SONGS:** "Montana" by Charles Cohan and Joseph E. Howard

**MOTTO:** *Oro y Plata*, or "Gold and Silver"

**FLOWER:** bitterroot

**TREE:** ponderosa pine

**BIRD:** western meadowlark

**ANIMAL:** grizzly bear

**DATE/RANK OF STATEHOOD:** November 8, 1889; the 41st state

**CAPITAL:** Helena

**AREA:** 147,039 square miles (380,829 sq. km)

**AVERAGE JANUARY TEMPERATURE:** 18°F (-8°C)

**AVERAGE JULY TEMPERATURE:** 68°F (20°C)

**POPULATION AND RANK:** 1,005,141; 44th (2012)

**MAJOR CITIES AND POPULATIONS:** Billings (106,954), Missoula (68,394), Great Falls (58,893), Bozeman (38,695), Butte-Silver Bow (33,730)

**NUMBER OF US CONGRESS MEMBERS:** 1 representative, 2 senators

**NUMBER OF ELECTORAL VOTES:** 3

**NATURAL RESOURCES:** coal, copper, gold, lead, petroleum, silver, talc

**AGRICULTURAL PRODUCTS:** barley, beans, cattle, hay, potatoes, wheat

**MANUFACTURED GOODS:** lumber and wood products; machinery for farming, construction, and mining

**STATE HOLIDAYS AND CELEBRATIONS:** Montana State Fair

# GLOSSARY

**bison:** a large North American animal with a big, shaggy head; short horns; and a humped back

**cattle:** cows, bulls, and steers that are raised for food or for their hides

**chuck wagon:** a covered wagon carrying food for cooking

**exhibit:** a display that shows something interesting to the public

**expedition:** a long journey with a specific goal

**flint:** a hard gray stone that sparks when steel strikes it

**fossil:** the preserved remains of an ancient plant or animal

**glacier:** a huge sheet of ice

**industry:** a group of manufacturing companies or businesses that brings money to a place

**moccasin:** a leather shoe once commonly worn by American Indians

**musher:** a person who drives a dogsled

**paleontologist:** a scientist who studies fossils and ancient life

**powwow:** an American Indian ceremony or social gathering

**prospector:** a person who searches for something, such as gold or silver

**refuge:** a place of protection or shelter

**replica:** a copy of something

**reservation:** land set aside by the government for special use

**tepee:** a cone-shaped tent made of animal skins

# FURTHER INFORMATION

Cunningham, Kevin. *The Sioux*. New York: Children's Press, 2011. Learn more about the Sioux American Indians who have called Montana home for thousands of years.

Gondosch, Linda. *Where Did Sacagawea Join the Corps of Discovery? And Other Questions about the Lewis and Clark Expedition*. Minneapolis: Lerner Publications, 2011. Read this book to learn more about the famous Lewis and Clark Expedition.

**Montana Dinosaur Trail**
http://www.mtdinotrail.org
Montana has many dinosaur museums. Read about them and order a Prehistoric Passport that you can take with you while touring all the spots.

**Montana Kids**
http://montanakids.com
This site has cool stories for you to read, activities and games for you to play, and fun things for you to see and do in Montana.

**National Park Service, Glacier National Park**
http://www.nps.gov/glac/forkids/parkfun.htm
Read about some fun activities you can do with your family at Glacier National Park. Learn how you can become a Glacier Junior Ranger.

Oachs, Emily Rose. *Montana*. Minneapolis: Bellwether Media, 2014. This book is full of fun facts about the Treasure State.

# INDEX

## PHOTO ACKNOWLEDGMENTS

The images in this book are used with the permission of:
© silky/Shutterstock Images, p. 1; © Cody Wheeler/
Shutterstock Images, p. 4; © Laura Westlund/Independent
Picture Service, pp. 5 (top), 26–27; © outdoorsman/
Shutterstock Images, p. 5 (bottom); © Andre Jenny/Alamy,
pp. 6–7; © Colton Stiffler/Thinkstock, p. 7 (top); © Robin
Loznak/Great Falls Tribune/AP Images, p. 7 (bottom); © Sue
Smith/Shutterstock Images, p. 8; © Connie Ricca/CORBIS/
Glow Images, pp. 8–9; © Eric R. Perlstrom/Thinkstock, p. 9;
© Audrey Snider-Bell/Shutterstock Images, pp. 10–11; C.M.
Russell/Library of Congress (LC-USZC4-7160), p. 11 (top);
© G Seeger/Shutterstock Images, p. 11 (bottom); © Casey
Riffe/Billings Gazette/AP Images, pp. 12–13; © Luc
Novovitch/Alamy, p. 13 (top); Library of Congress (LC-DIG-
ppmsca-17965), p. 13 (bottom); © puttsk/Shutterstock
Images, pp. 14–15; © Tom Reichner/Shutterstock Images,
p. 15 (left); © Laurent Le Gourrierec/Thinkstock, p. 15
(right); © S.R. Maglione/Shutterstock Images, p. 16;
© Dennis Donohue/Shutterstock Images, pp. 16–17;
© Claudio Beduschi/Glow Images, p. 17; © Tim Thompson/
Missoulian/AP Images, p. 18; © Walter Hinick/The Montana
Standard/AP Images, pp. 18–19; © Stockbyte/Thinkstock,
p. 19; © SuperStock/Glow Images, pp. 20–21; © John and
Lisa Merrill/Corbis/Glow Images, p. 21 (top); © Todd Klassy/
Shutterstock Images, p. 21 (bottom); © Radoslaw Lecyk/
Shutterstock Images, pp. 22–23, 23 (top); John C. H. Grabill/
Library of Congress (LC-DIG-ppmsc-02670), p. 23 (bottom);
© Robert Brown Stock/Shutterstock Images, pp. 24–25;
© Galyna Andrushko/Shutterstock Images, p. 24 (left);
© Laurin Johnson/Thinkstock, p. 24 (right); © Atlaspix/
Shutterstock Images, p. 27; © 6015714281/Shutterstock
Images, p. 29 (top); © Sarah Jessup/Shutterstock Images,
p. 29 (middle top); © Jason Maehl/Thinkstock, p. 29 (middle
bottom); © Anna Malanushenko/Thinkstock, p. 29 (bottom).

Front cover: The images in this book are used with the
permission of: © Larsek/Shutterstock.com, (bison); © Jack
A/Shutterstock.com, (glacier);© Steve Bower/Shutterstock.
com, (balloon); © Colton Stiffler/iStock/Thinkstock
(dinosaur); ); © Laura Westlund/Independent Picture Service
(map); © iStockphoto.com/fpm (seal); © iStockphoto.com/
vicm (pushpins); © iStockphoto.com/benz190 (corkboard).